ANNE FRANK

Life in Hiding

Anne and her parents walked all the way, in the summer rain, to the building at 263 Prinsengracht. The house had been constructed in the seventeenth century alongside the canal. Because the price of those early houses was determined by their width, Otto Frank's workplace was an extremely narrow building with steep steps leading to the upper floors. Behind the building facing the canal was a second building. It was connected to the first by an internal passageway. Anne had been here before, and she thought she knew the office and the warehouse where spices and herbs were stored. But when she walked up the familiar steep staircase, she was surprised to discover that a small door led to several additional rooms in the back building.

Who could guess that behind the door were two more floors with a total of four rooms, and an attic floor, too? It was here that the Franks and the Van Daans were going to hide.

ANNE FRANK

Life in Hiding

JOHANNA HURWITZ

Decorations by Vera Rosenberry

A Beech Tree Paperback Book
New York

Printed in the United States of America.
First Beech Tree Edition, 1993. Published by arrangement
with the Jewish Publication Society.

20   19   18   17   16   15   14   13   12   11

Library of Congress Cataloging-in-Publication Data

Hurwitz, Johanna.
    Anne Frank : life in hiding / Johanna Hurwitz ; illustrated by
Vera Rosenberry. — 1st ed.
        p.   cm.
    ISBN 0-688-12405-4
    1. Frank, Anne, 1929-1945—Juvenile literature.   2. Jews-
-Netherlands—Amsterdam—Biography—Juvenile literature.
3. Holocaust, Jewish (1939-1945)—Netherlands—Amsterdam—Biography—
—Juvenile literature. 4. Amsterdam (Netherlands)—Biography—
—Juvenile literature.   I. Title.
DS135.N6F7335   1993
940.53'18—dc20   92-28820
                                                       CIP
                                                        AC

The names of the occupants of the secret hideaway and of
their Dutch protectors that are used in this book are the
fictional names Anne chose for them. These are the same
names that are used in the published editions of
Anne Frank's diary.

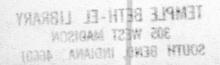

CONTENTS

Europe, 1943–44

ANNE
FRANK

Life in Hiding

1

Happy Birthday, Anne

June 12, 1942, was the thirteenth birthday of Anne Frank. Her home, at 37 Merwede Square in Amsterdam, was filled with flowers as Anne sat down to open her presents. She received books, jewelry, a game, and a puzzle. There were chocolates and other candies. Anne also received some money that she could spend as she wished. Right away, Anne made up her mind. She would buy herself still another book, one about Greek and Roman mythology. Anne was a lively girl with loads of friends. She loved to go skating and to play with her classmates, but she loved reading, too. Among the gifts, there was a book with a red-and-white-checked cover. Inside, the pages were blank. It was a diary in which Anne could record her own story.

Probably, Anne also received a poem that her father had written in honor of the event. It was a family tradition, and Anne and her older sister Margot looked forward to those verses that he wrote for them on special occasions. He wrote his verses in German.

The Frank family lived in Holland, but it was only natural for Otto Frank to write his poems in German. He had been born and educated in Germany. In fact, the whole family—both parents and Anne and Margot—had been born in Germany. During the First World War, Otto Frank had served in the German army and had become a lieutenant. When Otto married Edith Hollander in 1925, they settled in Frankfurt, Germany. He assumed they would live there for the rest of their lives. After all, Otto's ancestors had lived in that city as far back as the seventeenth century. In 1926, the Franks' first daughter Margot was born. Three years later, on June 12, 1929, their second daughter was born. She was named Annelies Marie. It was a long name for a baby, and before long she was just called Anne.

Although the Frank family was German, it was also Jewish. In 1929, Frankfurt was the home of about 30,000 Jews among a total population of 540,000 people. After Berlin, it was the second largest Jewish community in all of Germany. At one time, there had been rules singling out the Jewish people and forcing them to live in a separate area called the ghetto. But since the beginning of the nineteenth century, new laws said that the Jews were equal to all other people in Germany; they could live and work as they pleased. With such a long history of acceptance and opportunity behind them, it was no wonder that the Franks looked forward to a long and happy life in Frankfurt.

But even though 1929, when Anne was born, was a

time of celebrating for Otto and Edith Frank, it was not a good year for Germany. Many businesses closed, and, as a result, thousands of people were out of work. One-quarter of Frankfurt's population was unemployed.

A new political party called the National Socialist German Workers party—the Nazis—had been formed after the First World War. As times grew worse, more and more people supported this party. These supporters blamed the bad times in Germany on a weak government and on the Jews.

It was not the first time in history that the Jews were blamed for something they had not done. Anti-Semitism had come and gone before. Edith and Otto Frank and the other Jews around them hoped that, with time, this ill feeling toward them would be forgotten.

But as the economic situation got worse, the Nazis became stronger. In an election in 1933, Adolf Hitler, the party's leader, was elected as head of a government made up of several political parties. Two months later, he seized total power. All the other political parties in the country were outlawed, and those people who opposed the Nazi party were sent to prison camps.

With Hitler firmly in power, anti-Semitism became official government policy. Laws were passed that did not allow the Germans to shop in stores owned by Jews. It was forbidden for people who were not Jewish to consult a Jewish doctor or a Jewish lawyer. Furthermore, physical attacks against Jews in the streets were common.

By mid-April 1933, a law was passed stating that all public employees who had even one Jewish grandparent were to be fired from their jobs. Jewish teachers

3

were not permitted to teach in the schools. As Jews lost their jobs, there was more work for pure Christian Germans. The Nazis called these Germans "Aryans."

Suddenly the Franks found that they were not Germans after all—they were Jews, and, because of that, they were hated. Most of the Jews living in Germany tried to convince themselves that these new laws would not last. How could more than a hundred years of acceptance be undone in just a few weeks? It was difficult for men who had served in their country's army and had fought for Germany in the last war to believe that they were not true citizens. Surely the madness of the Nazis was just a passing phase in German history.

Some Jews, however, realized that Germany was no longer a safe place in which to live and to raise their families. And Otto Frank was one of them. In 1933, when the Nazis seized power, he left Frankfurt and went to Amsterdam, Holland. He had often gone there on business trips. There, he set up a branch of a German company. His wife and daughters joined him months later, and a new life in a new country began for Anne and her family.

Holland is famous for its great religious tolerance and acceptance of all people. In the seventeenth century, the Pilgrims, who were to become some of the first American settlers, traveled first to Holland before they boarded the *Mayflower* and came to the New World. And still earlier, in 1492, Jews fleeing from the Spanish Inquisition had also found a friendly home in Holland. By 1933, when the Frank family arrived in Amsterdam, there were more than 100,000 Jews living in Holland. Since half of that number made their home in Amsterdam, it was no wonder that some people called the city the "Jerusalem of Europe." And it was no wonder that Otto Frank was confident that he had made a wise choice in moving his family to Holland, away from the Nazis and the anti-Semitism of Germany.

To move to a new country and to learn a new language and customs are not easy. But Otto Frank's business thrived, and he made good friends among his Dutch colleagues. And Margot and Anne were so young that they adapted to their new home without problems. They learned to speak Dutch.

The girls were enrolled at the Montessori School, which was just a few blocks from their home. They quickly made friends. In Anne's class, there were thirteen other Jewish children. Some were refugees from Germany, just like Anne.

Although it rains 175 days a year in Amsterdam, life was sunny and happy for Anne and her family. The good times, however, did not last. The influence of Hitler and the Nazis began to be felt outside of Germany. It was the Nazi plan to conquer all of Europe. First, Austria was taken over by Germany. Next, Czechoslovakia was conquered by the Germans and was no longer an independent country. Then, on September 1, 1939, Germany invaded Poland. Two days later, France and Great Britain declared war on Germany.

Holland had been a neutral country during the First World War, and many Dutch people expected that during this new war Holland would again remain neutral. But the war was coming closer all the time. Within six months, Germany invaded Denmark and Norway. Then, on May 10, 1940, Germany invaded Belgium, Luxembourg, France, and Holland.

The invasion of Holland came as a complete surprise. The Dutch were unprepared to defend themselves against a country so much larger than they were. Within days, the country was forced to surrender. Holland was occupied by the Germans. Dutch government officials and the Dutch royal family fled to England.

For the rest of the Dutch people, there was no possibility of fleeing. Many Dutchmen were forced to go to Germany and work in the factories. Those who remained in Holland found themselves governed by new German laws. Just like in Germany, strict regulations that dealt with Jewish citizens were enforced. All Jews had to sew a yellow six-pointed star on their clothing.

Anne was forbidden to run errands for her mother, except between the hours of three and five o'clock in the afternoon. She could only go into stores that had the sign "Jewish shop." She could not be outside after eight o'clock at night, not even in her own garden. Anne and Margot could not go to the movies or play tennis or go swimming. They could not ride on a train, eat in a restaurant, or visit openly with their Christian friends. Wooden signs announcing "Voor Joden Verboden" ("Forbidden for Jews") were posted almost everywhere.

Perhaps saddest of all, twelve-year-old Anne was forced to leave the Montessori School. She wept when she said good-by to her teacher. Anne and Margot enrolled in the Jewish Secondary School. Although they were joined by their Jewish classmates, they left behind many good friends. And they were well aware that this change in their education was still another of the dreadful events that were going on throughout the country, events that affected them and the other Jews in Holland.

And it was all caused by the insane hatred that the German Nazis felt toward Jews.

Still, Anne's father tried hard to protect his daughters from fully realizing just how desperate the situation was for Jews. And that's why Anne's thirteenth birthday was celebrated with all the festivities that she had come to anticipate.

Anne was a good student and got along well with most of the teachers at her new school. But she often talked in class to her friends. One day, the math teacher became so irritated by Anne's constant talking that he gave her a special punishment. She had to write a composition about "a chatterbox."

Undaunted, Anne proved to her teacher that her words could flow as fluently on the page as they did when she spoke. She wrote that talking is a feminine characteristic, and although she might work to keep it under control, she did not think she could be cured. Furthermore, she wrote that her mother talked just as much as she did, and so being a chatterbox was undoubtedly an inherited characteristic.

The math teacher laughed at Anne's composition, and all was well until the next time Anne began to chatter in class. A second report was assigned, now entitled "Incurable Chatterbox." Again, Anne succeeded in filling the composition pages for her teacher. But when she still continued talking a few days later, he scolded her with disgust. "Anne, as punishment for talking, will do a composition entitled 'Quack, quack, quack, says Mrs. Natterbeak,'" he announced to the student. Everyone in Anne's math class roared with laughter, and Anne had to laugh, too. She was rescued from this ridiculous assignment by her friend Sanne, who offered to write a poem for Anne. The poem was about three baby ducklings who were bitten to death by their swan father because they chattered too much.

The math teacher read the poem aloud to the class and shared it with his other classes, too. After that, he ignored Anne's chattering in class. He knew he couldn't change her.

For a girl as bright and as imaginative as Anne was and who could express herself so readily on paper, a diary was a wonderful birthday gift. So when Anne discovered the red-and-white-checked book among her birthday gifts, she was delighted. She promised herself that she would write in the book regularly.

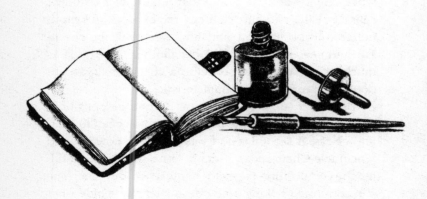

Even though she had several good friends—Lies and Jopie and Sanne—she considered the new diary to be her closest friend. She decided that she would call this new and private friend "Kitty" and that the entries she wrote in the diary would be in the form of letters. She would be able to tell Kitty personal things that she had never shared with her real-life friends or with her mother or her sister. She could write whatever she wished because it was unlikely that anyone else would ever read what she wrote. After all, Anne thought as she began to fill the blank pages of her diary, who would possibly be interested in the words of a thirteen-year-old schoolgirl? The first entry was dated Sunday, June 14, 1942. Anne began by describing her birthday.

2

A New Home

Less than a month after Anne's birthday, a postcard arrived at the Frank household. Sixteen-year-old Margot had received the dreaded summons from the Germans. The "call-up" meant that she would be taken away to work in a German factory. Worse still, there was much talk in the Jewish community about the concentration camps, where the Germans were deporting a steadily increasing number of Jews. Since no one ever returned to report on these camps, people could only suspect with dread what it would be like to live in one.

Now that the Germans controlled the country, it was impossible for Jews to escape from Holland. Since Otto Frank knew that he and his family could not leave Holland, he thought of an alternate plan. Rather than risk having his family sent away by the Nazis, he would arrange for them to hide somewhere in Holland. Other Jews he knew had already gone into hiding. It was called "diving."

Although the Germans controlled the country, many native Dutch people did not support them. They did not agree with the anti-Semitism of the Germans and felt great compassion for their Jewish neighbors. Some of these Dutch people helped the Jews by letting them hide in their basements, attics, or barns. Some Dutch families even took Jewish infants and young children into their homes and passed the children off as family members. Not only did these people share their rationed food supplies with the Jews, they also put their own lives at risk. If the Germans were to discover that a Dutch family was sheltering Jews, then that family, too, would be arrested and sent to a concentration camp. Nevertheless, thousands of kindhearted Dutch helped the Jews.

Very early in the morning on July 6, 1942, Anne was awakened. Following her mother's instructions, Anne put on layer after layer of clothing. It was not a cold day. But it was the day the family was going into hiding, and it was too risky to be seen carrying suitcases. Anne wore two undershirts, three pairs of pants, a dress, a skirt, a jacket, a summer coat, two pairs of stockings, sturdy shoes, a woolen cap, and a scarf. She must have looked very fat with all that clothing on as she walked down the street with her parents at 7:30 A.M.

Margot had already left with Miep, a typist who worked for the spice firm that Otto Frank had run. Anne didn't know where Margot and Miep were headed. And Anne didn't know where she was going as she walked with her parents out into the rain, each carrying a school satchel and a shopping bag filled with an odd assortment of possessions. She could not take her cat Moortje, but she knew that Moortje would be adopted by the neighbors without any problem.

As they walked along, Anne's parents confided their plan to their daughter. Although they were diving suddenly because of the call-up that Margot had received, they had been planning for this moment for many months. They would be joined by three other Jews: Mr. and Mrs. Van Daan and their fifteen-year-old son Peter. Mr. Van Daan had worked in Otto Frank's spice business. Amazingly, their hiding place would not be out in the country, but in Amsterdam. And even more amazingly, it would be in the building where Otto Frank had once had his office.

When the Germans occupied Holland, one of their regulations forbade Jews to control their own business. But even though Anne's father was no longer the director of his spice company, he was still closely associated with his former employees. And despite the propaganda against the Jews, these Christian employees remained loyal and devoted to their former boss.

Anne and her parents walked all the way, in the summer rain, to the building at 263 Prinsengracht. The house had been constructed in the seventeenth century alongside the canal. Because the price of those early houses was determined by their width, Otto Frank's workplace was an extremely narrow building with steep steps leading to the upper floors. Behind the building facing the canal was a second building. It was connected to the first by an internal passageway. Anne had been here before, and she thought she knew the office and the warehouse where spices and herbs were stored. But when she walked up the familiar steep staircase, she was surprised to discover that a small door led to several additional rooms in the back building.

Who could guess that behind the door were two more floors with a total of four rooms, and an attic floor, too? It was here that the Franks and the Van Daans were going to hide.

This clever scheme to hide in Amsterdam—under the very noses of the Nazis—could not have worked without the assistance of a few of Otto Frank's former employees—two older men, Mr. Kraler and Mr. Koophuis, and the two young women who worked in the office as typists, Miep Van Santen and Elli Vossen.

For many months, Otto Frank's loyal co-workers had been preparing for the arrival of their Jewish friends. The hidden rooms were filled with dishes, rugs, bedclothes, clothing, books, and furniture. There were boxes of canned food, too. Each item had been brought into the building secretly. Not only did these devoted friends have to be sure that the Germans were unaware of what they were doing, but they had to take care that the other workers at the business did not know either.

Mr. Kraler and Mr. Koophuis felt that it was important to involve as few people as possible in this scheme. The Germans were offering reward money to those who helped them find hidden Jews. So everyone had to be very cautious if the Franks and the Van Daans were going to hide successfully until the enemy was defeated.

The first days in hiding were busy. Because their move had taken place earlier than was originally planned, there was a great deal to be done by all of them. The boxes containing the Franks' possessions, which had been secretly sent ahead, were now waiting to be unpacked. Dark blackout curtains had to be made for all the windows so that no light would guide English and American planes flying overhead. But for the Franks, the curtains served another purpose. No one was to guess that these back rooms at 263 Prinsengracht were occupied. The workday ended at 5:30 P.M. People would become suspicious if they knew that the building was occupied afterhours.

The four rooms were divided up. Anne's parents had the larger room, just above the office. Next door was a small, narrow room that Anne and Margot were to share. At first, it looked bare and stark, not at all like their attractive rooms at home. But Otto Frank surprised Anne by showing her that he had packed her collection of picture postcards and magazine cutouts of movie stars. Using a pot of paste, Anne quickly covered the walls with her favorite pictures. Now, when she walked into her room, movie stars like Ginger Rogers, Deanna Durbin, and Greta Garbo were smiling at her. She also pasted up a picture of the Dutch royal family. How good it was to know that they, too, were safe from the Nazis.

There were many rules that Anne and her family had to follow if their hiding place was to remain secret. Although they had a bathroom and a kitchen with running water, during the day the water could not be used. That meant that the toilet could not be flushed and pots of water had to be filled for use during the day. Many people came regularly to the lower floors at 263 Prinsengracht to conduct business. These people must not hear any strange noises overhead. Anne and the others had to tiptoe about in bedroom slippers, talking softly and even smothering their coughs. It was a relief when 5:30 came and it was safe to flush the toilet and to speak out loud once again.

Yet, even at night, the hiders had to restrain themselves. It was quiet in the buildings all around them, and the Franks had to be careful in case their movements created suspicious echoes along the canal. But through the silence, one sound was constant. The Westertoren clock sounded every quarter of an hour. Otto, Edith, and Margot Frank didn't like that chiming at all. But from the start, Anne loved it. When she lay in her narrow bed at night and it was too dark to see her beloved pictures, the chiming of the clock was like a friend to her.

A week after the Frank family settled into life in the hidden rooms, they were joined by Mr. and Mrs. Van Daan and their son Peter. Mr. and Mrs. Van Daan occupied the room above that of Anne's parents. This room served as a kitchen and sitting room during the day. At night, beds were lowered from the walls for Mr. and Mrs. Van Daan to sleep in. Peter Van Daan slept in the small room adjoining his parents' room.

Anne had looked forward to the arrival of the Van Daans. She thought it would be loads of fun when they were all together. In her diary, she wrote to Kitty that living in the secret rooms was "like being on vacation in a very peculiar boardinghouse."

At first, it seemed like fun—two families cosily hiding together. They shared a dangerous secret, and together they felt safe in their secret annex. Mr. Van Daan reported on the rumors he had heard after the Franks had disappeared. Some of the neighbors said that the

Frank family had managed to flee to Switzerland. Others insisted that they had seen the Franks depart on a pair of bicycles. Still another woman was certain that the entire family had been taken away in a car by the Nazis in the middle of the night.

During the week that the Franks had been in hiding, more Jews than ever before had been arrested and sent away by the Nazis. No wonder the Franks were delighted to be together, safely out of sight of the Germans. The family would wait out the war together. And someday soon the Germans would be defeated and everyone could return home.

In the meantime, Elli Vossen's father, who was also employed by the spice firm, was let in on the secret of the people in the annex. Mr. Vossen was a clever carpenter. He devised a bookcase that was attached to the door leading to their rooms. It perfectly disguised the entrance to their hiding place. Now, certainly, no one could guess that anything was behind there.

The two families ate their meals together, everyone helping in its preparation and in the cleaning-up afterward. It was nice to have another young person around, even though Peter Van Daan, like Margot Frank, was quiet and didn't speak much. He had brought his cat Mouschi to the annex, which proved very useful. Rats had gotten into the stored bags of food in the attic, but Mouschi soon took care of the rodents.

After a while, however, this cosy safety of the annex was not enough. The hiders could not go outside for fresh air or a walk. They had to look at the same walls and the same faces over and over. Their only trips were to the offices below their rooms. They could go there at night after the staff had departed for the day.

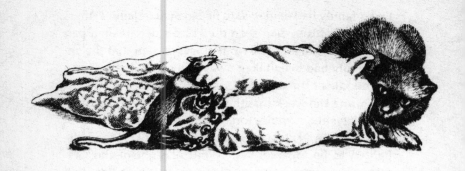

Lack of variety in their days made life tiresome and boring. Otto Frank planned a full schedule of studies for the three young people. When the war was over, he did not want them to be behind in their schoolwork. Besides, studying French verbs and doing arithmetic helped pass the time. Elli, from the office below, sent for a correspondence course so the young people could study shorthand. It would be a useful skill for Anne and Margot to have in the future.

Still, the sameness of the day's routine remained boring. Everyone grew tense and easily irritated. Sharp words were often exchanged, and chatterbox Anne discovered that she was, more often than not, the cause of arguments.

Mrs. Van Daan criticized if Anne did not want to eat a large portion of a detested vegetable. Also, when Anne tried to joke and make comments to relieve the unpleasant mood at mealtime, Mrs. Van Daan was not amused. "It's absurd that Anne's so frightfully spoiled," Mrs. Van Daan said frequently. "I wouldn't put up with it if Anne were my daughter."

Anne was thankful that she was not Mrs. Van Daan's daughter, but her own mother and sister often found fault with her behavior, too. She discovered that it was not easy to be thirteen while being locked away in a hiding place with others who seemed old and serious and unsympathetic so much of the time. Luckily, Anne had her diary.

Even if no one else could understand how she felt and why she acted the way she did, at least Kitty never scolded her. So day after day, when her studies were completed and her chores were done, Anne would find herself a private corner and would tell Kitty what had been occurring in the secret annex.

In November 1942, after the Franks and the Van Daans had been in hiding for four months, it was decided that there was enough room and food in the annex to hide one more person. Mr. Koophuis and Mr. Kraler both agreed that it was "just as dangerous for seven as for eight" to be hidden in the building. A conference was held, and several Jewish friends were considered. It was not easy to select just one individual. Finally, Miep carried a message to Albert Dussel, a dentist whom both families knew.

Dussel arrived and moved his possessions into Anne's small room. He would share it with Anne, and Margot would sleep with her parents. While the eight occupants of the secret annex sat around the table drinking coffee, Dussel told them all that had been happening in Amsterdam during the months they were in hiding. It was news that Miep and their other guardians had avoided speaking of so as not to distress their Jewish friends.

Dussel said that night after night, the German police—the Gestapo—had driven about the city ringing doorbells and inquiring if there were Jews present. When Jews were discovered, they were put into trucks and taken off to Westerbork, a big prison camp that had been set up in Holland. There they had their heads shaved and were forced to live under extremely primitive conditions.

When she heard these stories from Dussel, Anne realized that despite the hardships of being confined in such a small hideaway, she was living in paradise compared to those Jews who had not managed to hide from the Nazis. Anne sat down and wrote in her diary. She knew she was very lucky.

3
Hiding

Two things made the long days in the annex more bearable for Anne and the others— daily visits from the office staff and listening in the evening to the radio reports from Britain about the progress of the war.

Almost every noon, Miep or Elli or one of the men would enter the hideaway for a short while, join the hiders at the table, and take a small portion of soup as the families ate lunch. The presence of one of these guests often kept the others from arguing among themselves or criticizing Anne's behavior. A new face in the middle of the day was a lively diversion, and Anne looked forward to it. She called the visitors "the soup eaters."

Also, Miep and Elli made every effort to devise unexpected treats for the occupants of the annex. The two managed to secure an unending supply of books and newspapers. Anne had always loved to read. But now that she was confined to the hideaway, books were more important to her than ever before. When she was reading, she forgot about the war and the Germans and being locked up in this hiding place.

And Miep was able to supply Anne with more paper when Anne filled all the pages of her birthday diary. First, Miep got her a blank school notebook, and when that, too, became filled with Anne's writing, Miep supplied her with empty ledger books from the office.

Somehow, despite rationing and shortages, Miep and Elli managed to secure shoes and clothing for Anne, who continued to outgrow the garments that had been brought into the annex for her. Young people need fresh air and exercise and nourishing food to grow. Yet, even with all of those items in short supply, Anne, Margot, and Peter kept growing. Otto Frank measured their heights, which were indicated by pencil marks on the wall.

From constantly reading in dim light, Anne's eyesight suffered. She needed a pair of glasses. For a while, everyone seriously considered having Anne temporarily leave the hiding place to go with Mrs. Koophuis to see an optician. The idea was terrifying. How wonderful to go outside again—into the real world—even if only for a couple of hours. But how frightening to think about what would happen if the Germans discovered her. In the end, it was decided that the risk was too great.

Whenever there was a special occasion such as a birthday or a holiday, Miep and Elli brought surprises for everyone in the attic. A little extra butter meant that they could bake a cake. And, even with a dentist looking on, everybody savored the extra sugar or candies that the young women could sometimes manage to find.

In December, the Franks, the Van Daans, and Dr. Dussel celebrated Hanukkah. Like the Jews in ancient times who lacked holy oil, the eight hiders did not have enough candles to burn. So for just ten minutes, they symbolically lit a wooden menorah that Mr. Van Daan had made. But they sang the holiday songs. It was not like the joyful Hanukkahs that they had had before the Germans came, but at least they could still celebrate the holiday. The Germans had not succeeded in taking that away from them.

One evening, as a special treat, Miep and her husband Henk stayed overnight in the hideaway. To Anne, overnight guests made her peculiar insulated existence seem more like the normal life of the past. She had gone to the wedding ceremony when Miep and Henk had gotten married. How long ago that seemed now. During the night, Anne and the other hiders slept peacefully. But Miep and Henk, unaccustomed to the tensions of sleeping in the secret annex, could hardly sleep at all.

They listened in the dark to the sounds of cars going over the bridge and along the canal. Each car might have been driven by the German police. Suppose they were all discovered? It was a sound and a possibility that those in the secret annex had grown used to. Another time, Elli stayed as the overnight guest in the annex. She, too, was in terror for hours and could not sleep.

Every evening, the hiders gathered around the radio. Softly, they turned the dial to the forbidden station that broadcast the news from England. The Germans did not report their losses in the war, but the English kept the

Dutch people informed. It had been Hitler's plan for the Germans to conquer and rule all of Europe. But now, as the war raged on and the American armed forces had joined the English and the Russians, the German army was beginning to suffer severe defeats. Every night, the Franks, the Van Daans, and Dr. Dussel could hear the hundreds of planes flying over Holland on their missions to bomb Germany. The broadcasts from England told everyone just what was really happening. Otto Frank had hung a map of Europe on the wall, and with colored pins he marked the progress of the war.

On Wednesday evening, September 8, 1943, they listened with great excitement to the news that German-occupied Italy had surrendered to the Allied forces. If the American soldiers could overcome the Germans in Italy, couldn't they free the Dutch from their Nazi captors, too? It was news like that which gave Anne and her family hope. Already they had been in hiding for fourteen months. It was just a matter of time until they would all be free again.

Sometimes the hiders allowed themselves to dream about what they would do first if they were free to return to their old life. Anne wrote in her diary that both Margot and Mr. Van Daan longed for a leisurely bath with plenty of hot water. Mrs. Van Daan said that she wanted to eat cakes filled with cream. Anne's mother wanted a cup of real coffee. Peter said he wanted to go to town and see a movie. And Dr. Dussel wanted to be reunited with his wife. Anne's father wished he could visit Elli's father, who, they had learned, was very ill with cancer. As for herself, Anne had so many dreams that she didn't know where to start. She wanted her family to have its own home again and the ability to move about freely. And, perhaps most of all, Anne wanted to return to school. She missed both the guidance of her teachers and the companionship of her classmates.

Another time, Anne and her sister discussed what they wanted to do when they were older and the war was over. Margot said that she would like to go to Palestine and become a midwife. Anne decided that she did not want to settle down. She would rather travel all over the world as a journalist. And even though she understood Margot's wish to live in a land of Jews, Anne felt a fierce loyalty and devotion to her adopted homeland. After the war, she wanted to become a Dutch citizen. If necessary, she would write directly to the queen.

The forbidden radio broadcasts often brought Anne and the others news of the Dutch Resistance. Despite the possibility of severe punishment by the Germans, thousands of brave Dutch men and women were secretly working to undermine their enemy. They set fire to the German department of the Labor Exchange and to the Registrar's Office. By destroying German records, the Resistance created chaos and stopped some people from being arrested. Even though many of the Resistance leaders were shot by the Germans, other brave people continued to work in secret.

Throughout these long months, Anne wrote frequently in her diary. Sometimes she wrote in her bedroom, if Dr. Dussel was not there. Other times, she went to the attic to write. By writing, she was able to vent some of her anger and impatience toward her parents. At fourteen, an age when a girl begins to expect some independence from the adults around her, Anne was under constant surveillance. Margot and Peter Van Daan also were subjected to this. But they were quieter and more reserved than Anne, and seemed able to suffer in silence. Anne needed an outlet for her emotional exuberance. She was a chatterbox who was unable to chatter in their cramped quarters. But when she wrote her letters to Kitty, she experienced a sense of release for her feelings. The diary also gave Anne a bit of privacy amid her crowded surroundings. Everyone knew she was keeping a diary, but no one knew just what she was writing. When she wasn't writing in it, Anne stored her diary in her father's old leather briefcase.

One evening during a radio news broadcast, it was suggested that a collection of diaries and letters written during the war be published when the fighting was over. These words fueled Anne's thoughts of becoming a journalist when she grew up. She spent much of her spare time writing little imaginative stories about dwarfs and elves. She also wrote essays based on memories of life before the war. But, mostly, Anne wrote in her diary, keeping her imaginary friend Kitty informed of all that was taking place both in the annex and in her thoughts.

One day Anne wrote that she had dreamed in the night of her old friend Lies Goosens. Lies seemed to Anne to be a symbol of the sufferings of all her girl friends and of all Jews. "When I pray for her, I pray for all Jews and all those in need," she wrote.

To Kitty, Anne could also complain about the awful food they ate. Food was in short supply throughout Holland, and ration coupons were necessary for purchasing everything from bread and butter to meat and potatoes. Elli and Miep had managed to get extra ration coupons through the black market in order to purchase food for the eight in hiding. Both the local baker and the man who supplied them with fruit and vegetables were aware that the unusual amounts of food that Miep and Elli bought were for divers. But neither man asked questions. The less one knew, the better.

Still, the quantities were severely limited, and often there was no variety. Once, they had to eat sauerkraut for lunch and supper for several days in a row. Another time, they had endive day in and day out. "Endive with sand, endive without sand, stew with endive, boiled or *en casserole*," Anne complained to Kitty.

Dried beans and peas were also a constant in their diet. Several sacks of beans were stored in the hideaway. One day, it was decided to put the sacks up in the attic, out of everyone's way. The job of moving these sacks was given to Peter Van Daan.

As he was pulling one of the sacks up the stairs, the bag's seam burst and a shower of the hard brown beans came pouring out. "There were about fifty pounds in the sack and the noise was enough to waken the dead. Downstairs they thought the old house with all its contents was coming down on them," Anne recorded in her diary. Thankfully, there were no customers in the office below to hear this loud and unexpected noise. And after a moment of great fright and suspense, Anne and Peter were able to laugh heartily with relief at the absurdity of the accident. Anne stood at the bottom of the stairs "like a little island in the middle of a sea of beans." Together they began to pick up the small and slippery beans, and for days afterward everyone was still retrieving them from all the corners into which they had rolled.

An accident like this would not have been funny if anyone who didn't know about the hiders had been in the building. At all times, their presence had to be kept secret. More than once, they were almost discovered.

In February 1943, the owner of the building sold it without informing either Mr. Kraler or Mr. Koophuis. The new owner and an architect arrived to inspect the property. With great presence of mind, Mr. Koophuis managed to show them around the building, and when they came to the connecting passageway that led to the area outside the secret annex, Mr. Koophuis claimed that he had forgotten the key. Luckily, the new owner was satisfied with what he had seen. He did not return to check any further.

Because of the severe shortages in Amsterdam, the crime rate increased considerably. Desperate people looking for food or items to sell broke into buildings. Several times at night or over long weekends, burglars broke into the office or the warehouse at 263 Prinsengracht. There was always the chance that the burglars would overhear those in hiding and betray them to the German police. Worse still, the police might come to investigate the burglaries and discover the hiders.

Anne's heart beat rapidly as she thought about these possibilities. She knew that should she and the others ever be discovered, their wonderful saviors Miep, Elli, Mr. Kraler, and Mr. Koophuis would be in grave trouble, too. And although she was basically an optimist, she could not help but write in her diary, "Again and again I ask myself, would it not have been better for us all if we had not gone into hiding, and if we were dead now and not going through all this misery."

Anne had always been close to her father, whom she affectionately called "Pim." She felt far less close to her mother, whom she found to be constantly critical of her. And although she was only three years younger than Margot, they were so different that Anne did not feel close to her either. Margot was reserved and serious, tidy and careful—all the things that Anne's mother wanted Anne to be. No wonder the two sisters were not close. One day in January 1944, Anne wrote to Kitty, "My longing to talk to someone became so intense that somehow or other I took it into my head to choose Peter."

Despite months of living so close together, Peter's shyness had prevented him from becoming close to the two sisters. But Anne began to seek him out. She had been thirteen when she and her family had entered the hideaway, but now she was going on fifteen. It is no wonder that she was attracted to this young man, two years her senior. Peter, in turn, found himself more and more attracted to Anne's lively ways. Her humorous comments and generally positive outlook brightened his days. Before long, the two teen-agers developed strong crushes on one another.

In another time, another place, two young people like Anne and Peter would have gone to the movies together and stopped to buy ice cream. They would have taken walks in the park or gone skating. Instead, they escaped to the attic of the hideaway and spent long hours talking. In the attic, they could leave the window open, and, when the sun shone through, they could sit on the floor and pretend that they were at the beach. There was no sand or water, but there was a bit of light and companionship. Sometimes Anne thought she was in love with Peter. And, like the visits from the office staff and the exciting radio broadcasts, her feelings for Peter helped make the last months in hiding more bearable for Anne.

4
Caught

From the time that Anne and her family had hidden at 263 Prinsengracht, there had been the constant dread of discovery. Everyone listened continually for the sound of footsteps and a pounding on the door. The Gestapo (the German police) were searching everywhere for Jews. When would they discover the eight hiders? However, with the passing of weeks and months in the secret annex, a sense of security had developed. Of course, there were moments of great fear. A burglary in April 1944 really frightened everyone.

At first the people in the annex did not know if the noises they heard were made by burglars or by the police. They did not want to be discovered by either. They sat in pitch blackness as they listened to steps nearby. It was the police, who had come to investigate an attempted burglary. The hiders heard the secret door being rattled from

31

the outside. What should they do? Fearfully, they whispered about destroying the forbidden radio that they had.

"They will find Anne's diary," Otto Frank said.

Someone suggested that the diary be burned. "Not my diary," Anne declared passionately. "If my diary goes, I go with it!" The diary was not burned, and, luckily, the divers were not discovered.

When the incident passed, they managed to look back on it and laugh. The war news on the radio was getting better and better. And so, once again, the hiders relaxed.

On June 6, 1944, called D-day in history books, the combined Allied forces, under the command of American general Dwight D. Eisenhower, crossed the English Channel to France to begin liberating occupied Europe from the Germans. Those in the annex heard the news at eight o'clock in the morning and discussed it over breakfast. Afterward, Anne wrote in her diary, "We don't know yet, but hope is revived within us. . . . Oh, Kitty, the best part of the invasion is that I have the feeling that friends are approaching."

And as the news of the Allied attack continued to be broadcast, Anne began to fantasize. Perhaps by September or October she would no longer be in this hiding place. Perhaps she would be home again and studying at school.

On July 15, 1944, Anne wrote in her diary, "I still believe that people are really good at heart. . . . I think that it will all come right, . . . that peace and tranquility will return again."

So with every reason to feel optimistic, the sudden arrival on the morning of Friday, August 4, 1944, of the Gestapo was all the more shocking and unexpected. How was it that after more than two years of hiding successfully from the Germans, the hiders were suddenly discovered?

It is believed that one of the warehouse staff guessed that Jews were hiding on the premises and betrayed them to the police. Perhaps he needed the reward money he knew he would get. Perhaps he believed the Nazi lies of Aryan superiority and wanted to rid his country of Jews. It is hard to know or to understand what would make one person betray others.

Suddenly, the moment that they all had been dreading for so long had become a reality. The Gestapo told the hiders to pack some clothes quickly. They were all under arrest. It did not take long for the hiders to gather the knapsacks that they had kept in readiness for the one day they had hoped would never come. A police officer searched for valuables and took Otto Frank's money, the family's silverware, and the menorah. He looked eagerly inside the briefcase that Otto Frank held, for he hoped to find still more valuables inside. He shook out the contents and was disgusted to see that the case contained nothing but some worthless notebooks and papers. At least the briefcase was useful. The officer took it to carry the silverware. And as the Franks, the Van Daans, and Dr. Dussel walked out of the rooms that had been their home for so many months, they stepped on the papers that had dropped from the briefcase.

There was no crying or yelling. They were numb with shock. They walked quietly, as they had always walked during the daytime in the annex. They went down the steep staircase and into a waiting van. The notebooks and papers remained on the floor. They were

ANNE FRANK

the pages that Anne had been so busily writing over the past two years—her diary and her little stories and essays. And they were left behind because the Gestapo officer thought they were worthless.

In addition to the eight Jews, the police took Mr. Kraler and Mr. Koophuis. But Miep and Elli had not been arrested.

The ten prisoners were taken to Gestapo headquarters, where they were locked in a room together. Otto Frank whispered to Mr. Koophuis about how bad he felt that this good friend had been arrested because of being kind to Jews. But Mr. Koophuis said, "Don't give it another thought. It was up to me, and I wouldn't have done it differently."

The Gestapo questioned both Mr. Koophuis and Mr. Kraler, and the two men remained silent. They had nothing to tell the police. Although he spent a few weeks in prison, Mr. Koophuis was released because of ill health. Mr. Kraler, who was stronger, was sent to a forced labor camp. Some months later, he managed to escape.

The fate of the eight Jews was not as good. After a few days, they were taken to the railroad station and transported to Westerbork, the camp in eastern Holland where Dutch Jews were sent before they were moved to the German extermination camp, Auschwitz. It was a terrible time for them all, and yet Anne was fascinated by the views of meadows and villages that she saw from the train windows. After so many months of seeing the same thing, a train ride—even a train ride to a prison camp—seemed like a special treat.

At Westerbork, they were housed in barracks that

held 300 prisoners. Everyone dressed in blue overalls with a red bib and was given wooden shoes that did not fit. The men had their heads shaved.

The prisoners were awakened early and at five each morning were sent to work. Children were assigned to the cable shop, and the adults worked at breaking up old batteries and salvaging the parts that could be used to make new batteries.

Despite the indignities of the situation, the poor food, and the long work hours, Anne was happy during this period. It was as if she were free. After two years, there were so many new people for the friendly chatterbox to meet and speak with. And after all those months of peeking longingly through the window, she was at last outside, breathing fresh air, and able to walk about. It was almost like a holiday.

On September 3, 1,000 people, including the eight hiders, were loaded onto a freight train. Although they were not aware of it, it was to be the last transport of Jews to leave Holland for dreaded Auschwitz. During the past months, close to 100,000 Jews had taken this same route from Westerbork to Auschwitz in German-occupied Poland.

Three nights after Anne and her family set out, the train arrived in Auschwitz. Immediately, they were separated—women to the left, men to the right. Now, Anne, Margot, and their mother had their heads shaved, too. And identification numbers were tattooed on their arms.

Jews from all over Europe found themselves together in the barracks. The little Dutch group stayed together and tried to give each other strength and courage. They knew that they would be made to work until they became too ill to continue. Then they would be sent to the gas chambers and killed. But they remembered, too, that the Allied forces were coming closer. If only they could hold out a bit longer, they might see the end of this hell. The war could not continue for many more months.

But Anne and Margot did not remain at Auschwitz long. Less than two months later, on October 30, while their parents remained at Auschwitz, the sisters were put on still another train and sent to the camp in Bergen-Belsen, Germany. Against her will, Anne was being brought back to the land of her birth. The trip took many days, and the prisoners suffered from hunger and thirst. Some died along the way.

Auschwitz had been horrible. But even though the food was bad, it was distributed regularly. Their barracks had been crowded but were kept clean. At Bergen-Belsen, there was neither food nor water. The barracks were so crowded that for the first few nights, Anne and Margot slept in a tent on the ground. But the autumn weather was rough, and one night during a storm the tent blew down. After that, they found a space in a crowded, filthy barrack. Under such terrible conditions, the prisoners in increasing numbers came down with typhus or typhoid fever. During that winter of 1944–1945, first Margot and then Anne became ill with typhus.

However, a miraculous event did take place. One of Anne's closest childhood friends, Lies Goosens, whom Anne had dreamed about when she was in hiding, was imprisoned in another section of Bergen-Belsen at the same time that Anne was there.

Lies was more fortunate than Anne. Because Lies's

family had managed to get passports to go to South America shortly before they were arrested, they were assigned to barracks for "neutral foreigners." They were permitted to receive occasional Red Cross packages containing food and clothing. Despite this, both of Lies's parents died in the camp.

When Lies heard that her friends Anne and Margot Frank were at the camp, she went to the barbed-wire fence that separated her area from theirs and called softly into the darkness, "Is anyone over there?"

The voice that responded was that of Mrs. Van Daan. Lies asked her to give a message to Anne, and a little later the two friends were reunited in the night, separated still by the barbed wire. Anne shivered as they spoke together, and Lies was shocked at her friend's emaciated appearance. She could see that Anne was starving. Lies told Anne to come back to the same spot the next evening and that she would bring her something.

But the next night, when Lies threw a bundle containing a woolen jacket, some crackers, some sugar, and a tin of sardines to Anne, she could hear only cries and screams from the other side. Someone else had managed to catch Lies's gift. Deprived of life's necessities, each prisoner fought for her- or himself. Disappointed, Lies promised to try again the following night. She could bring only a pair of stockings and some crackers. But this time, Anne was successful in catching the bundle. It was the last time the two friends saw each other.

Not long afterward, at the end of February or the beginning of March 1945, Margot Frank, who had been gravely ill, died of typhus. Anne was not informed of

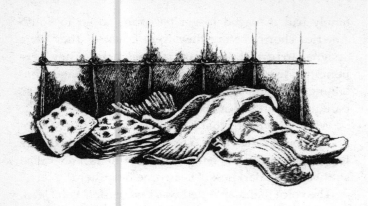

her sister's death, but she must have guessed it. She, too, was now very sick. Her courage and her love of life were not strong enough to help her small body fight the deprivations of food and water. There was no medicine for sick prisoners, and will power was not a good enough weapon against typhus. Soon after her sister's death, Anne died, too.

Anne Frank died less than two months before the war ended, three months before her sixteenth birthday. But despite her youth, she would become one of the most famous names in twentieth-century history.

5

The Diary

The war was over!

On May 8, 1945, the German army unconditionally surrendered. Although fighting continued in Asia, for all those people in Europe who had suffered under the German occupation, this was the day for which they had been waiting and fighting for more than five years.

Millions of people had been killed during these terrible years. This included the systematic murder of millions of civilians—men, women, and children. And 6 million Jews were among the victims of Adolf Hitler and his Nazi regime.

It took time for the world to learn the full extent of the Nazi savagery. Pictures of concentration-camp survivors show people that resembled skeletons. And photographs of mass graves with hundreds of naked bodies piled on top of one another still stun everyone. As the survivors were freed, wherever they went, they brought their horror stories with them.

They came searching for their families. Otto and Edith Frank had remained at Auschwitz when Anne and Margot were sent to Bergen-Belsen. But because males and females had been separated, it was only after the Russian soldiers had freed the prisoners that Otto Frank learned the dreaded news. His wife had died four months before the end of the war—on January 6.

Anne's father had seen Mr. Van Daan as the latter walked to his death in the gas chamber at Auschwitz. Later, Otto Frank learned the tragic fate of the others who had hidden with him in the annex. Albert Dussel, Peter Van Daan, and Mrs. Van Daan had all died. And he learned about his daughters, Margot and Anne—both dead, too. They were all part of the gruesome statistics.

Of the 120,000 Jews who had lived in Holland in 1940, 106,000 were murdered by the Nazis. Of the 14 Jewish children who had been in Anne's class and expelled from the Montessori School because of Nazi laws, only 3 survived the war. And of the 8 in hiding at 263 Prinsengracht, only Otto Frank was still alive.

When Otto Frank arrived in Amsterdam, traveling by way of Russia and France, he returned to the house on Prinsengracht Canal. There he learned that the two men who had protected and cared for the occupants of the secret annex, Mr. Koophuis and Mr. Kraler, had returned home safely to Amsterdam from the prison camps.

Miep gave the grief-stricken Otto Frank the notebooks and papers that she had discovered strewn about the room after the Gestapo had ransacked the secret hideaway. For the first time, Otto Frank read the letters to

Kitty that Anne had written. From time to time in the past, Anne had read a passage or two aloud to the others. Still, her father was stunned by the contents. Here was a full picture of what it was like to hide for twenty-five months. Reading his daughter's perceptive and candid portrayal of the hiders, Otto Frank saw them all live again.

Anne's father decided that he would have Anne's diary privately printed as a memorial—not just to Anne, but to the entire family. However, a Dutch university professor of modern history, who happened to see a typed copy of the diary, urged Otto Frank to publish it formally. That way, more people would be able to read the diary and learn the story of those years in hiding.

Thus, in June 1947, *Het Achterhuis* (The Secret Annex) was published in Amsterdam. It was the name that Anne herself had chosen when she jotted in her diary on May 11, 1944, that after the war she wanted to write a book about these wartime experiences.

Among Anne's papers was a sheet with names that she had prepared. They were fictional names to be given to the other people in this book of hers. Otto Frank substituted these names in the text. He also edited out some personal passages that he felt Anne herself would have omitted had she been alive to complete her book. There were a few spelling errors and mistakes in grammar that were corrected. Otherwise, the diary was printed as Anne had written it over the days and weeks and months between her thirteenth birthday and the last entry on Tuesday, August 1, 1944—three days before the discovery of the hiders and their arrest by the Gestapo.

Several printings of the book quickly sold out. People

read the diary and identified with Anne. She became a symbol of all the young people who were destroyed by Hitler's armies during the Second World War. The extermination of 6 million Jews is a hard concept to grasp. Who were they? What were they like? How did they react to the life around them? In Anne's diary, one soon knows Anne very well. Even before one reads the book, one knows her fate. But, still, one reads on to learn more about this lively, imaginative girl. And knowing her, it is impossible not to care for her and to admire her courage and humor. When the book concludes, the reader has lost a new friend. And in feeling that loss, the reader can begin to understand about all the other war losses, too.

In 1950, three years after the first Dutch printing, Anne's diary was published in a German translation. Some German booksellers were afraid to show the book in their store windows. Who knew how people would react to this little book about a young, innocent girl's life and death at the hands of their countrymen and -women? The book also reminded people of all the other inhuman crimes committed by the Nazis.

Despite the misgivings and fears of the booksellers, the book rapidly found an audience. More than 900,000 copies were soon sold in the German edition. That same year, the book was published in France. In 1952, the diary was published in both England and the United States. Eleanor Roosevelt, widow of President Franklin Roosevelt, who had led the United States throughout the Second World War, wrote an introduction to this new edition. Mrs. Roosevelt stated that the diary was "one of the wisest and most moving commentaries on war and its impact on human beings" that she had ever read.

In time, more than fifty different translations of the diary were published throughout the world, and more than 18 million copies were sold. Since several people may read a copy of a book, there is no way of estimating just how many millions of people have read Anne's letters to Kitty in the past forty years since the book was first made available to the world.

And many people have seen the play and the movie that were based on the diary. Anne has inspired artists who have used many different art forms. Sculptors have created statues and busts of her. Marc Chagall illustrated with lithographs a deluxe French edition of Anne's diary. A ballet and several contatas and requiems are also based on Anne's diary.

The name "Anne Frank" has been given to dozens of schools throughout the world, as well as to youth hostels and homes and clubs for young people. The Montessori School that Anne attended in Amsterdam and was forced to leave when the Germans took control of the city has changed its name to the Anne Frank School. And in Bergen, West Germany, the city where Anne died in the concentration camp, there is an elementary school named for her.

A forest of over 10,000 trees has been planted in Anne's name in Israel. In Belgium, a new rose was cultivated and named *Souvenir d'Anne Frank*. And in Anne's adopted homeland, Holland, a country known for its beautiful tulips, a new tulip was named for her, too.

Also in Holland, the Anne Frank Foundation has been established. It sponsors educational projects and exhibits to foster understanding and to fight anti-Semitism and racism of every kind.

Anne's favorite photograph of herself, which had been taken in May 1939, was selected by her father for the book jacket. This picture and others that were included in the published book and on a Dutch postage stamp have made Anne's face, like her name and her story, known to millions.

Today, the house at 263 Prinsengracht does not need to hide anyone. Instead, it has become a museum where visitors of all faiths and from every country come to view the rooms where Anne and the others hid from the Nazis. There, one can still see the fading photographs of Anne's favorite movie stars. One cannot help but realize with irony that not one of those stars has a face or a name that is as well known today as Anne's.

IMPORTANT DATES

1914–18   War World I. Otto Frank serves in German army.

1919   Establishment of Nazi Party (National Socialist German Worker's Party).

1925   Marriage of Otto Frank to Edith Hollander in Frankfurt, Germany.

1926   Birth of Margot Frank, Anne's older sister.

1929   June 12: Birth of Annelies Marie [Anne] Frank.

1933   January: Adolph Hitler elected leader of German government.

1933   March 23: Hitler seizes total control of power.

1933   April 1: Official boycott of all Jewish shopkeepers, doctors, and lawyers is declared.

1933   April 11: All public employees with at least one Jewish grandparent are fired from their jobs.

1933   Otto Frank goes to Amsterdam and establishes a business. He is joined by his wife and children.

1938   March 12: Germany annexes Austria.

1938   September 29: The Munich Treaty. France and
        Great Britain agree to the occupation of *Sude-
        tenland* (Czechoslovakia).

1939   September 1: Germany invades Poland.

1939   September 3: France and Great Britain declare
        war on Germany.

1940   April 9: Germany invades Denmark and
        Norway.

1940   May 10: Germany invades Holland, Belgium,
        Luxembourg, and France.

1940   May 15: Holland surrenders to Germany.

1940   August 27: Germany, Italy, and Japan form a
        pact.

1941   December 7: Japan bombs Pearl Harbor, Ha-
        waii (the American Naval Base in the Pacific).

1941   December 8: The United States declares war
        on Japan.

1941   December 11: Germany and Italy declare war
        on the United States.

1942   June 12: Anne Frank's 13th birthday. She is
        given a diary.

1942   July 6: The Frank family goes into hiding in
        Amsterdam.

Important Dates

1942   July 13: The Van Daan family joins the Franks in hiding.

1942   November 16: Dr. Albert Dussell moves into the hiding place, too.

1943   July 10: Allied troops land in Sicily, Italy.

1944   June 6: D-Day. Allies land in Normandy, France and begin liberation of France.

1944   August 1: Last entry in Anne's diary.

1944   August 4: Occupants of the secret hideaway are arrested. Within a few days they are sent to Westerbork Concentration Camp.

1944   September 3: Italy signs secret armistice with the Allies.

1944   September 3: The eight hideaways are sent to Auschwitz Concentration Camp.

1944   September 11: American Army reaches the German border.

1944   October 30: Margot and Anne are sent to Bergen-Belsen Concentration Camp.

1945   February-March: Margot and Anne develop typhus. Margot dies. Anne Frank dies shortly after her sister.

1945   May 5: Liberation of Holland.

1945   May 8: German Army surrenders unconditionally.

1945   August 14: Japanese surrender and the end of
        World War II.

1947   *The Secret Annex* (Het Achterhuis), Anne's
        diary, is published in Holland.

AUTHOR'S NOTE

In 1952, when Anne Frank's diary was published in English, I was the same age that Anne had been when she was writing it. My great-grandparents had come to America from Germany, and, coincidentally, my last name was Frank, too. In reading Anne's book, I felt that I had discovered a new sister whom I had never met before. Furthermore, her story of the persecution of Jews, hiding, and death could so easily have been my story had my relatives remained in Germany instead of emigrating.

Before I began writing this book, I made a trip to Amsterdam with my daughter. The two of us walked along the same narrow streets that Anne had walked as a young girl. Then we went to 263 Prinsengracht to see the rooms where Anne and her family hid. There were other tourists present, but we shut our eyes and imagined the small, shabby rooms with only the eight secret inhabitants present.

"I want to go on living even after my death," Anne wrote on one of the pages in her diary. "And therefore I am grateful to God for giving me this gift, this possibility of developing myself and of writing, of expressing all that is in me."

One does not need to share a religion or culture or name with Anne Frank to be moved by her story. World War II now seems far in the past. If Anne were alive today, she would be the age of your grandmother. But even though she did not live to have children or grandchildren, she has a world of sympathetic and loving friends. As long as there are people to read, her words and her name will live on.

Anne Frank will never die.

May 1988

INDEX